D1586269

NEVER A STRANGER

Acknowledgements

The Bible has been quoted from several translations: The New International Version, the New American Bible, The Revised Standard Version; in a few rare cases, the translation is my own, but the translation most frequently used is the New Jerusalem Bible, published and copyright by Darton, Longman & Todd Ltd., and Doubleday and Co. Inc.

Cover photograph : Icon of the Baptism of Jesus (original in the church of Reconciliation, Taizé).

NEVER A STRANGER

God's Otherness in the Light of the Gospel

by

Brother Emile of Taizé

Les Presses de Taizé

First published 1987 by A.R. Mowbray & Co. Ltd, Oxford
© Ateliers et Presses de Taizé, 1991
ISBN 2-85040-112-9

Contents

I ascended higher than myself; the Word was still far above me. And, inquisitive explorer that I am, I also descended deeper than myself, only to find that the Word was deeper still. If I gazed outwards it was only to realize that the Word is beyond everything external to myself; and if I looked inwards, I saw only that the Word is deeper within than I am myself. At this point I recognized the truth of a text I had read: «In Him we live and move and have our being».

Saint Bernard

Jesus is at home in the innermost heart of others.

Pierre Rousselot

ABBREVIATIONS

The following abbreviations have been used in biblical references:

Gn	Genesis
Ex	Exodus
Ps	Psalm
Is	Isaiah
Jer	Jeremiah
Mt	Gospel of Saint Matthew
Mk	Gospel of Saint Mark
Lk	Gospel of Saint Luke
Jn	Gospel of Saint John
Rm	Romans
1 Co	1 Corinthians
Ga	Galatians
Ep	Ephesians
Phil	Philippians
Col	Colossians
Heb	Hebrews
Rv	Revelation

Chapter and verse are separated by a comma, e.g. Mk 1,11 refers to Chapter 1, verse 11.

INTRODUCTION

God is the Other, the Altogether Other, whose thoughts are not our thoughts, and whose ways are not our ways; this can never be stressed enough nor recalled too often. The danger of projecting is ever present. To imagine God using ourselves and our experiences as starting-point is to fashion an idol and clothe it in our desires. To understand God as Other, as the One who brings «what no mind has conceived» (I Co 2, 9), is the first essential for faith.

But calling God the Other, and even more the Altogether Other, can give rise to questions and awaken anxiety. For these words «Altogether Other» carry the meaning of an unfathomable otherness which we cannot conceive, and cannot measure. Here we are no longer faced with the otherness whose role in human friendship and love is extolled by philosophers and psychologists. What is involved is an otherness for which we have no common denominator. Now it is only natural to wonder what a relationship with someone Altogether Other could possibly mean. If God is Other, can he still be encountered? Can he still be close? Close to what we are, close to the aspirations of the human heart? These questions take on capital importance when we consider that the Gospel is not content with inviting us to converse with God, it urges us to seek his will unceasingly, to live in his sight and to refer to him constantly. How then can we still say that we are free? Is another's overseeing of my life acceptable? Can I still be myself? Won't this relationship be alienating?

Other than other

When we call God the Other and want to avoid the danger of projection, it is easy to slip imperceptibly towards another projection, more subtle and more difficult to discern, but just as harmful, namely, to transfer to God our human experience of

otherness. To imagine God's otherness
from the standpoint of our own — to conceive God as other in the way people are
other, as I am in relation to my neighbour.
This transference is particularly fatal when
difference is understood as distance. There
are differences between persons which en-
hance relationships, there are others which
are burdensome, causing painful misun-
derstandings and grievous failures. Understanding otherness as distance falsifies our
relationship with God: the Most High becomes the most distant.

A misunderstanding of God's otherness disfigures him. If God is simply that
other who meets me as a stranger, it becomes difficult to understand that his will
is not arbitrary. It becomes difficult to
maintain that the accusation of alienation
levelled at the Christian faith is without
foundation.

Misconceiving the otherness of God
obscures our reading of the Gospel. It is
by no means rare nowadays to find readers
deeply attached to those pages of the Gospel which show the humanity of Jesus, but
who reject, or at least are embarrassed, by

the passages which reveal him as the Other. Is this not for fear of losing his nearness? As Son of man, resembling a man (Ph 2, 7), as one of us, in the likeness of sinful flesh, (Rm 8, 3), Jesus is close to us; will he still be so if we attribute to him the glory of God and admit his sinlessness?

Nothing is more fatal to faith than opposing otherness and nearness in the God of the Gospel. Every page of the Gospel and the mystical tradition gives the lie to this opposition. God is Other but not as we are other. He is not other in the same way that I am for my neighbour. His otherness never means distance. If he is the Altogether Other, it is because he is still other than other. For God is not of the same kind as us nor does his being add up to make one more with ours, he is not a digit in the sum of creation or of what exists [1]. Other, but never a stranger, Other, «deeper within me than my innermost depths». The Other who lives within us, and still more, the Other in whom «we live and move and have our being» (Ac 17, 28).

To escape from making projections is no easy matter. But on this question the Christian faith is not pessimistic; it rests on one simple certainty, that when God speaks about God everything is right. The Gospel is this word of God about God. And this word is Someone whose life and joy and mission are precisely to reveal God to us by speaking our human language and communicating to us all we need in order to understand him. «The Word became flesh» (Jn 1, 14). «At many moments in the past and by many means, God spoke to our ancestors through the prophets; but in our times, the final days, he has spoken to us in the person of his Son» (Heb 1, 1-2). Christ reveals God not only by the words he utters but also by his gestures and his actions, to the point of being able to say: «Anyone who has seen me has seen the Father» (Jn 14, 9). Now the Gospel reveals to us how God can be at the same time other and close. The more we discern his true otherness, the more his nearness stands out. The Altogether Other is the Altogether Near. It is also because he is other than man, that Christ is incomparably close. When that has been understood, everything that makes Christ more than a man becomes attractive. It becomes possible to love his glory. And then all the passages which show him to be the Other, are no longer to be feared. His otherness allows us to have an inkling of an inexpressible nearness. When we have comprehended that God is never a stranger, never a purely external presence, but that he is «deeper than our innermost depths» then we can realize that his life within us is the very foundation of our freedom.

*
* *

When he wrote *The Idiot*, Dostoyevsky had realized that there is no one closer to us than the Other. That is one of the secrets of that mysterious character, Prince Myshkin. A figure expressing otherness, a figure of Christ[2], in any case a figure who reminds us of Christ, he is the only one in Nastassia's life of suffering who

18

understands her: «He is the first man I've ever come across in my life in whom I can believe as a true and loyal friend. He believed in me at first sight, and I believed in him» [3].

God would not be nearer us, if he were in our image, as we might sometimes be tempted to suppose. It is also because he is the Other that he is close to us, that he understands all and forgives as no one else forgives.

*

*   *

When we quote Isaiah's words: «My thoughts are not your thoughts, and your ways are not my ways» (Is 55, 8), we too often forget that Isaiah's purpose was not to speak of an inaccessible stranger; what the prophet intended was to make known a God «rich in forgiveness», a forgiveness beyond anything his people could imagine. Contemporary men and women are longing, often unconsciously, for this forgiveness. Without it, without this forgiving look, more generous and accepting than we are ourselves, all of us are like orphans. We turn inwards on ourselves in a desperate search. Athirst, but ignorant of the source that can slake it. Is there not a need today, perhaps more than ever before, for Christians to point the way to the Other?

This book was written with the hope of responding to this need. It looks at the God of the Gospel, at certain key moments of Christ's life and some central aspects of his message to see how God reveals himself as other and close at one and the same time. Close at the very point where he seems most other, and other when he shows himself most human.

NOTES:

1. «If God is transcendent, then nothing is opposed to him, nothing can limit him or be compared with him: he is "wholly other" and therefore penetrates the world absolutely.» HENRI DE LUBAC, *The Discovery of God*, ET Alexander Dru, New York, PJ Kenedy & Sons, 1960, p. 97. «But God! In nothing is he the same. Not only Other, not only Altogether Other, but as Father Monchanin used to say, Altogether Other than other. And this allows us to say that he is Non-Other.» FRANÇOIS VARILLON, *L'humilité de Dieu*, Paris, Centurion, 1974, p. 40.

2. «Idiot» in Greek means peculiar, other, different. With *The Idiot*, Dostoyevsky constructs «a complete novel, beginning with a character who intervenes as the absolutely other», a «description of the eruption of this Other into the world». JACQUES ROLAND, *Dostoïevski, La question de l'Autre*, Verdier, Coll. «La nuit surveillée», Paris 1983, p. 110. It is known that Dostoyevsky's intention in writing *The Idiot* was to draw a figure of the absolutely beautiful. Dostoyevsky wrote: «There is only one face which is absolutely beautiful – the face of Christ...» *Correspondence*, *III*, Paris, Calmann-Lévy, p. 173.

3. *The Idiot*, Penguin Classics, 1955, p. 186.

I

The Holy One Among Sinners

On the banks of the Jordan, John the Baptist awaits the Messiah. What will he look like? How can he be recognized? John does not know. But he does know that he is to prepare the Messiah's coming, and that this coming will be the decisive intervention of God in history. John is preparing his nation for that day. He preaches and practises a baptism of repentance for the forgiveness of sins (Lk 3, 3). The sinners and all who recognize that their lives need to be changed come streaming to him.

The Baptizer is an austere figure. His life-style is one with the austerity of his words. The man is consistent: «This man John wore a garment made of camel-hair with a leather loin-cloth round his waist,

and his food was locusts and wild honey»
(Mt 3, 4). His message is clear: the people
must be ready to receive the One who is
coming, for when he does come, it will be
to take those who are ready. His coming
will produce separations and divisions:

«Even now the axe is being laid to the root of
the trees, so that any tree failing to produce good
fruit will be cut down and thrown on the fire»
(Mt 3, 10).

«His winnowing-fan is in his hand; he will
clear his threshing-floor and gather his wheat into
his barn; but the chaff he will burn in a fire that
will never go out» (Mt 3, 12).

The Messiah who will appear will be
totally other. John however is right to announce the decisive nature of the coming
intervention; he has received his commis-
sion from God. But the nature of this intervention, what it will consist of, John cannot
imagine. It is not in his power to guess the
face of the coming one. When he sees
Christ coming towards him to ask to be
baptized, the Baptizer is astounded: «Then
Jesus appeared: he came from Galilee to
the Jordan to be baptised by John. John

tried to dissuade him, with the words, « It is I who need baptism from you, and yet you come to me!» (Mt 3, 13-14). In Matthew's Gospel a single word, «then», separates the everlasting bonfire and the very humble coming of Jesus, as if the evangelist wanted to emphasize the contrast. There is nothing spectacular about the arrival. Christ comes from Galilee, a district of no reputation and which does not impress his contemporaries (Jn 1, 46). The one who comes is not faceless; he bears a common name, Jesus, and no threatening fire is associated with him.

Although totally other, Jesus is the one John recognizes. Jesus is both the one expected and the Other who is disconcerting. And with regard to all of the Scriptures which prepare his coming, Jesus maintains the same relationship: he fulfils and he surpasses all that has been announced.

To John, Jesus answers: «Let it be so now: it is proper for us to do this to fulfill all righteousness» (Mt 3, 15). «Let it be» words which were to appear later in the same Gospel, in the parable of the wheat and the weeds (Mt 13, 24-30) precisely in order to convey that the time had not yet come to separate the good from the sinners, the weeds from the wheat. Jesus did not come to divide but to stand beside, to be in solidarity.

As an act of solidarity with sinners, the baptism of Jesus is perfect. Not that Jesus had sinned. The thought that Christ would be closer to us if he were a sinner like us can be attractive. But a moment's reflection is enough to show us that the contrary is true[1]. It is precisely because he is sinless that Christ can stand in solidarity with us. For if sin consists in always acting out of self-interest, to the detriment of others and of God himself, there can be no solidarity in that. Sin is separation from God but also desertion of our neighbour, refusal to take responsibility for another. The Old Testament, with deep insight, had realized this already: after the Fall, Adam blames Eve and Eve blames the serpent (Gn 3, 12-13). Jesus comes to be with sinners, to carry the weight of their guilt, to bear the sin of the world. And his coming into our world repairs the torn unity of the human family.

Because he is sinless, Jesus is other than us. We have no knowledge of what it means always to do the will of the Father (Jn 8, 29). No human being has ever had that experience. The state of sinlessness is unknown to us. But the otherness of Christ does not consist in distance from us. It makes greater nearness possible. It is because he is other that he can draw so near and be in such solidarity with us. His otherness is nothing but perfect love. To express this kind of love, the Gospel employs an unusual word: *agapè*. It describes the attitude that seeks not its own interest, but only the good of the other. «God is a subsistent altruism» wrote Maurice Zundel[2].

In placing himself in solidarity with sinners, Jesus expresses the holiness of God. John is not mistaken when he announces that Christ is the one who baptizes in the Holy Spirit (Mt 3, 11), but his holiness is not as John imagines. It neither judges nor condemns. There is no rigidity in it. It does not consist in creating separation; it impels Jesus to join sinners and share their lives. Holiness is not made relative by this behaviour; it is lived to the full. Jesus embodies a new type of holiness, a new expression of holiness is found in him. Holiness for Jesus is to stand alongside, it means «being with», even unto death. Jesus, empty of all selfishness, holy, mingles with sinners to bear the sins of the world.

At his baptism, at the dawn of his mission, Jesus, the Holy One of God, comes «to gather together into unity the scattered children of God» (Jn 11, 52). So it is, that, without any contradiction, the Holy One can go down into the water with the sinners . And so the Father can recognize his Son, the one who can fulfil his eager desire to be close to human beings, to love them and to spare no effort that not one should be lost (Mt 18, 14): «You are my Son» he says, «you are my joy» (Mk 1, 11).

Notes:

1. ALBERT VANHOYE, *Prêtres anciens, prêtre nouveau selon le Nouveau Testament*, Paris, Ed. du Seuil, coll. «Parole de Dieu», 1980, p. 133, 135.

2. RENE HABACHI, *Trois itinéraires... un carrefour*, G. Marcel, M. Zundel, et Pierre Teilhard de Chardin, Québec, Les Presses de l'Université Laval, 1983, p. 73.

II

Forgiveness

It is always risky to apply human words to God, particularly to his forgiveness. To avoid understanding forgiveness from our poor human experience, always limited, often ambiguous, we must carefully weigh our words. We must be ready to affirm that God forgives, to see that his forgiveness is free of our limitations in order to discover that he is forgiveness itself. There is perhaps nothing more essential for people of our day than to enter into the discovery of another kind of forgiveness, one which springs from the source of pure love.

Christ is the expression of God's forgiveness. Anyone looking at him discovers forgiveness at its clearest, forgiveness untarnished. Jesus' relationship to forgiveness is more than that of a messenger. He is not on the outside of what he is announcing. He is unlike the prophets who, in order to accept and accomplish their mission, have to overcome their first reactions of fear and feelings of total impotence: «I am slow and hesitant of speech» (Moses), «I am only a child» (Jeremiah). With Jesus, spontaneous reaction is one with his mission. His personality is intimately connected with his message. For him, to reveal God's forgiveness means to be himself. God's forgiveness finds expression in his gestures and his speech. But Jesus is more than a translator:

«A translator transposes; but Jesus does not transpose, he does not reproduce a heavenly model; he himself, on earth, performs acts which belong to God alone: he forgives sins (Mk 2, 5-7). But he performs these acts only by virtue of a power and in the name of his mission. There is in him perfect harmony between the being and his function, between the person and the messenger — not

32

the harmony of the messenger who gives himself completely to his mission and consecrates his life to it, like John the Baptist, the bridegroom's friend; but the immediate, original harmony of him who is himself only when he appears as having come from another... » [1]

Because he is the perfect expression of God's forgiveness on earth, because he is the presence of the Other in our world, the forgiveness Jesus brings is astonishing. It was because of his way of expressing forgiveness that John sent from prison to ask Jesus: «Are you the one who is to come, or are we to expect someone else?» (Mt 11, 3). Someone else? What John is actually saying is that he expected someone more in conformity with his expectations, someone more like ourselves. While the devout Jew had to shun contact with sinners, Jesus seeks it; he seeks the society of sinners, rejoices with them, invites himself to their meals (Mk 2, 15) and makes it his duty to visit them in their homes (Lk 19, 5). Is this really the one who is to come?

The answer Jesus gives John seems to enter into his anxiety: «Go back and report to John what you hear and see: the blind recover their sight, cripples walk, lepers are cured, the deaf hear, dead men are raised to life, and the poor have the good news preached to them. Blessed is the man who finds no stumbling block in me!» (Mt 11, 4-6). Jesus lists the messianic signs and shows their fulfillment in him. But why speak of stumbling? Certainly not because of the healing and the raising of the dead. The stumbling block is the Good News to the poor, among whom Jesus includes sinners. Plainly Jesus is saying: «Happy are you, John, if you do not stumble because of me, because of how I treat those sinners who are also the poor».

Jesus is conscious of acting differently from the religious men before him. He knows that his attitude does not square even with the noblest of their religious ideas. He knows that his behaviour is disconcerting and he realizes its dangers and difficulties. To receive this new wine, new wineskins are essential (Mk 2, 22).

Not that the Old Testament was silent about forgiveness. John the Baptist certainly knew the texts about mercy, and he himself received the sinners who came to be baptized. But in the Old Testament and for Jews in the time of Christ, God limited his forgiveness to those who had already made a move of conversion towards him. The absolute originality of the Gospel is that Jesus goes towards sinners just as they are, before they have shown any sign of repentance or any desire to change their lives. It is he who takes the initiative. Here is a reversal which is his alone. And «in this reversal lies the whole of Christianity»[2]. If he perseveres on this road which is so incomprehensible for John, if he seeks the company of sinners, if he enjoys being with them, it is not because he is trying to be original in some way or to show approval of their conduct, but it is because Jesus must express on earth what God is feeling. If he does not conform to human expectations, it is because he is the presence of the Other in our world.

Jesus explains what God feels in several parables, particularly in three which Luke has grouped together (Lk 15). These parables are inspired by happenings in everyday life, specifically the loss of something precious and the joy of finding it again. Is Jesus not referring to something human and normal? Yes and no.

As in many of the parables, though the beginning is natural and true to human life, there comes a moment when the parable turns into the unusual[3] and the presence of the unusual means that we are leaving our human experience to enter the world of the Other, the world of God. What is expressed now is valid only for God. The figure of the shepherd was doubtless familiar to the inhabitants of Palestine, perhaps evoking the prophecies of the Old Testament in which God himself promises to be the shepherd of his people (Ezechiel 34), but had there ever been a shepherd like the one Jesus talks about? He leaves ninety-nine sheep exposed to all possible dangers and goes off to look for the lost one until he finds it. A woman who finds a coin again is of course delighted but does she really call on all her friends and neighbours to share her joy? There are other instances, often bound up with forgiveness. Nothing was more familiar to Jesus' listeners than employers and workers. But what employer would give a full day's pay to one who had worked only for an hour? (Mt 20, 1-15). Creditors and debtors were also familiar characters of everyday life. But where would you find a creditor who totally forgoes enormous sums of money? (Mt 18, 27).

The parable of the Lost Son (Lk 15, 11-32), more than any other, develops the double theme of normal human reactions and extravagance. The framework is certainly human life. A son leaves home, squanders what his father has given him and then returns. It is at the moment when the father welcomes him that the unusual takes place. Not that a welcome from a loving father is inconceivable. But that the return of the one who squandered the family fortune should trigger such a celebration: «Quick! Bring out the best robe and put it on him, put a ring on his finger and sandals on his feet. Bring the calf we have been fattening, and kill it; we will celebrate by having a feast, because this son of mine was dead and has come back to life; he was lost and is found» (Lk 15, 22-24).

Better still, Jesus added a detail which must have surprised his listeners:

37

on seeing his son returning, the father, moved with compassion, «ran» towards him (v. 20). In Palestine an older man never runs. This one did, and as soon as he held his son in his arms, he «clasped him and kissed him», interrupted his son's speech of apology and gave himself up to the joy of making him welcome.

God's feelings? The three parables are clear: immense joy. «There will be more rejoicing in heaven... » (Lk 15, 7). «There is more rejoicing among the angels of God... » (v. 10). And the joy of the father of the lost son knows no bounds.

Now what we have here is certainly human. But this is a humanity so complete that there is nothing like it on earth. Absence of any resentment, such pure joy, compassion strong enough to make the father run, love so constant in spite of lack of response, these all lead us to think that this is more than a human welcome. Extravagance, a characteristic of transcendence, reveals God the totally Other, but his otherness is described as overflowing humanity. The forgiveness of the Other as described in the Gospel allows us to discover that God alone is perfectly human.

When the Gospel speaks of forgiveness, it is with a joy and a lightness of touch which shows that this forgiveness comes from elsewhere. This forgiveness has nothing of our condescension. It humiliates no one. It reveals to every individual their immense value, and shame itself is overcome in the immeasurable joy created by the return of the sinner, the rejoicings of restored communion.

When Isaiah spoke of a God rich in forgiveness, several centuries before Christ, he immediately added: «my thoughts are not your thoughts and your ways are not my ways» (Isaiah 55, 7). God is revealed as the Other, by the quality and immensity of his forgiveness.

NOTES

1. JACQUES GUILLET, *The Consciousness of Jesus*, ET Edmond Bonin, New York, Newman Press, 1972, p. 67-68.

2. *Ibid.* p. 64.

3. See PAUL RICŒUR, *Listening to the Parables: Once More Astonished*, Christianity and Crisis 34, 1975, p. 304-308; and H. RIESENFELD, *Unité et Diversité dans le Nouveau Testament*, Paris, Cerf, Coll. Lectio Divina, 1979, p. 85-87, 90.

III

The Father Who Sees in Secret

The God who is Altogether Other, Jesus calls «Father». And immediately we seem to be treading more familiar ground. But when we look more closely at the meaning Jesus gives to the word Father it all becomes less certain, and soon it is evident that in discovering God the Father we also begin to know the Altogether Other.

Jesus constantly refers to the Father as the source of his words and his actions (Jn 8, 28-29). He lives by the Father (Jn 6, 57), in order to make his Name known (Jn 17) and accomplish his will (Mt 18, 14, Jn 6, 39). For Jesus the essential is always to do what he sees the Father doing (Jn 5, 19); his teaching is not his own but the Father's who sent him (Jn 12, 49-50; 14, 24). Because of the Father, he is never alone (Jn 8, 29; 16, 32). Jesus lives with his eyes upon the Father. He enters into his Passion so that the world may know that he loves the Father (Jn 14, 31). Saint John is not the only one to see the life of Jesus in this way. Luke sets the life of Jesus between two mentions of the word Father: the first at the beginning of his life: « Did you not know that I must be in my Father's house? » (Lk 2, 49), and for the last time on the cross: « Father, into your hands I commit my spirit » (Lk 23, 46).

Jesus is amazingly sure that he knows the Father, and more than that, not only does he know him, but he is conscious of responding perfectly to what the Father expects (Jn 8, 29). This certainty shines through in his words, in his every action, in the forgiveness he brings, in his healings and very powerfully in his prayers, where Jesus addresses God as « Abba ». This means much more than Father. The word conveys complete familiarity, perfect intimacy. Before Jesus no one had ever dared address God in this way.

But if Jesus constantly refers to the Father as the explanation of his person and his actions, never does he speak of him to his disciples as a reality they already know. The Father is the Altogether Other, the Unknown who must be discovered through Jesus, by setting out in his footsteps, finding out where he lives (Jn 1, 38-39). In John's Gospel, Jesus never says «Your Father» until after the resurrection (Jn 20, 17).

In the Gospel, God is not merely compared with a father as in the Old Testament. He is Father absolutely and he is the Father of Jesus. The Father is known by Jesus alone and only he can disclose him: «Everything has been entrusted to me by my Father; and no one knows the Son except the Father, just as no one knows the Father except the Son and those to whom the Son chooses to reveal him» (Mt 11, 27).

The Father is unknown to men; he is unlike human beings. It is imposssible to know him by thinking of the past — even the deepest experience of fatherhood would not be enough, only opening oneself to the newness of the coming Kingdom enables us to begin to enter into relationship with him: «Our Father... may your Kingdom come» (Mt 6, 9-10)[1]. A Father who lives in the future, unheard of in the earthly experience of fathers. But though the Father is the Altogether Other, when Jesus reveals him, we are not summoned to a distant deity. Although he is Altogether Other, the Father is not far from us. Jesus shows him constantly active in creation, with a concern and care exceeding anything possible for humankind. The tiniest detail matters to him and is the object of his attention. Nothing is too small. He counts our hairs, is concerned with clothing the grass of the fields and feeding the birds of the air (Lk 12, 7, 24-28). The Altogether Other is not for Jesus a kingly majesty centred on itself, but a Father, concentrating on the good he can do. Concern for the littlest one is ever present (Mt 18, 10). Every time Jesus evokes the Father's otherness, it is to let us have a sense of a goodness and a love far beyond all human imagining: «If you, then, evil as you are, know how to give your children what is good, how much more will your Father in heaven give good things to those who ask him!» (Mt 7, 11). The Father's otherness makes infinite caring possible.

Reading the Sermon on the Mount, we too often forget that several sayings of Christ reveal first and foremost the identity of the Father:

«If someone wishes to go to law with you to get your tunic, let him have your cloak as well. And if anyone requires you to go one mile, go two miles with him. Give to anyone who asks you, and if anyone wants to borrow, do not turn away. You have heard how it was said, You will love your neighbour and hate your enemy. But I say to you, love your enemies and pray for those who persecute you; so that you may be children of your Father in heaven, for he causes his sun to rise on the bad as well as the good, and sends down rain to fall on the upright and the wicked alike» (Mt 5, 40-45).

All these verses suggest unheard-of generosity. Giving without counting the cost, without calculating, characterizes the Father's actions. The disciples of Jesus are called to mirror him in the the world.

Because the Father is other, a closeness unexperienced by human beings enters our world. Because he is Altogether Other he is not limited to an external relationship. As the Altogether Other, he can be the Altogether Close and together with his Son make his home within us (Jn 14, 23). «It is because God is transcendent that he is immanent in his creature».[2] For Paul there is only «one God and Father of all, over all, through all and within all» (Ep 4, 6).

Otherness and nearness, two realities united in a remarkable phrase of Jesus: «Your Father who sees in secret». «With this sentence the New Testament revelation reaches an absolute peak. It unites the Father's understanding of humanity with divine judgment, the closeness of confident trust and the most rigorous inaccessibility»[3]. The allusion to secrets which God will one day reveal recalls the Judgment (Rm 2, 16; I Co 4, 5; 14, 25). But the transcendent Judge of history is «your Father». And what he is most concerned about seeing and appreciating is all the good people can do unconsciously.

The Father sees in secret but not as a spectator of human life. He is not spying on man. To realize how the Father sees without life ever becoming merely a spectacle to him, we must understand that he is the Altogether Other. Altogether Other is not simply other or different but Other than other, never a stranger[4]. The Father sees in secret but he does not violate human privacy: he is its maker and he dwells there. It is his gaze resting upon me that allows me to be myself, and makes me discover my deepest identity: «You received the spirit of adoption, enabling us to cry out, Abba, Father! The Spirit himself joins with our spirit to bear witness that we are children of God» (Rm 8, 15-16).

The feeling that someone is watching you can be intolerable. Oppressive when that look judges you and seems to be focused on your mistakes, creating anguish and fostering rebellion if it deprives you of your freedom. But the Father does not look at us in that way. His is a look of love which brings us to life, better than our own or any other appraisal. For there is also a look that can set us free, that can deliver us from the way we scrutinize ourselves, from the need to evaluate our personal progress and our worth, or from despair at our failures. In a novel by Paul-André Lesort, a character finds this other kind of look in his wife Isabelle:

«For a long time I needed a mirror much more than I ever thought I did. Why this need beyond that of self-satisfaction or self-accusation, whatever their obvious role could be? I thought it necessary to see myself as I really am. But if by this the illusion of self-sufficiency is dispelled, a truth more subtle than illusion is dispelled also. The truth of love which actually makes us other than our own view of ourselves. The natural view of the self in the mirror of actions and memories nourishes despair, cynicism or magic. It was from Isabelle that I learned, (but forgot again so many times) that we are infinitely more than what we are» [5].

There is a look that makes us realize that «we are infinitely more than what we are». An infinitely generous look in which it is possible to breathe, to relish life again and to overcome self-disgust. Such is the look of the Father who sees in secret. When Jesus tells his disciples to give up looking at the value of their deeds, their charity and their fasting (Mt 6, 1-6, 16-18), he is inviting them to live under that look. In the look which expresses: «You are my Son, you are my joy» (Mk 1, 11), Jesus is continually enfolded, and to share it, and to allow others to discover it, was why he came (Jn 15,11).

NOTES:

1. «If we follow the suggestion that prophecy is turned toward and looks for the fulfillment to come, toward the eschatological banquet, is it not necessary to go so far as to say that the figure of the father is itself entailed by this movement and that it is not only the figure of the origin – the God of our fathers, within the realm of the ancestor – but the figure of the new creation?» PAUL RICŒUR, *The Conflict of Interpretations: Essays in Hermeneutics*, Ed. by Don Ihde Evanston IL: Northwestern University Press, 1974, p. 489.

2. FRANÇOIS VARILLON, *L'humilité de Dieu*, Paris, Centurion, 1974, p. 109.

3. W. MARCHEL, *Dieu Père dans le Nouveau Testament*, Paris, Cerf, coll. «Lire la Bible» 7, 1966, p.86-87.

4. FRANÇOIS VARILLON writes: «The God of Christian faith is not that other who can be counted among his creatures. He is not even the Altogether Other. He is Altogether Other than the other, and therefore also the Non-Other. And yet I am not identical with him: he is not the Same. Neither Other nor the Same. But Transcendence of love which implies otherness and that is more immanent to me that my own immanence.» *Op. cit.*, p. 72-73.

5. PAUL-ANDRÉ LESORT, *Vie de Guillaume Périer*, Ed. du Seuil, 1966, p.226.

50

IV

In Distress I Am at His Side

Suffering awakens doubts about the nearness of God. Can we still call the one who allows it «Father»? Is he not a God who is indifferent? It is impossible to avoid these questions.

Jesus did not put forward any theory about suffering. He made no conjectures. Nor did he enter into the arguments about cause and effect into which people tried to draw him (Jn 9, 2). He discouraged his disciples from seeking an explanation in the past, as if suffering could be punishment for a sin. When face to face with someone suffering, Jesus did not try to explain: he was, says the Gospel, deeply moved (Lk 7, 13). The Gospel shows him impatient to

51

heal and to comfort (Lk 13, 10-16). If the words of Jesus are true: «Anyone who has seen me has seen the Father» (Jn 14, 9), then it is impossible to imagine a God indifferent to suffering.

«In distress I am at his side», says God in a psalm (Ps 91, 15). «Immanuel, God-is-with-us» writes Saint Matthew (1, 23) and he shows the Christ child reliving a painful page of his people's history: the exile into Egypt. God with us, to the point of crying out with human beings, through his Son: «My God, my God, why have you abandoned me?» God is never a spectator of human suffering. He is infinitely close.

When suffering and death drew near, threatening his very life, Jesus did not react with stoical impassivity. The Gospel accounts do not hide the depths of his distress. His «soul is troubled» (Jn 12, 27). «Terror and anguish» took hold of him (Mk 14, 33). To struggle against this state of mind, like a man in need he asked for human company, for his friends: «Wait here and stay awake with me» (Mt 26, 38).

In the darkest hour of that night there fell from the lips of Jesus a word of light,

«Abba», «Father» (Mk 14, 36). Very little, two syllables only, but enough to introduce a brightness that transforms the situation, enough to reject evil's claim to be in charge. Like an appeal to what is greater, more concealed than evil, but not less strong, not less present: the Father's love and his gracious plan which Jesus knows can be nothing but love for his Son, and forgiveness for people. The word of a little child who knows that he is perfectly safe in his father's hands.

This word of trust at the very heart of the prayer of Jesus sheds light on the petition which follows: «Let your will be done, not mine». To commit oneself to what the Father wills does not mean consenting to a fatal destiny, regretfully admitting the inexorable, implacable quality of events. On the contrary, for Jesus it meant expressing his attachment to and dependence on a will which is always life-giving, going forward in the certainty that love will have the last word, however unclear the way. This certainty Jesus does not cling to for himself alone; his hope embraces humankind, he has accepted this hour for all.

Abba-Father is not only said by Jesus as he watches carefree birds in the sky or the splendour of the lilies. The name is used and holds fast even when evil seems most powerful: Abba, the certainty of a presence in the darkest hour. The Risen Christ still prays «Abba» today in the prayer of women and men who, frail as they are, assert that life has meaning and there is a joy that no one can take away.

V

No One Has Ever Spoken Like This Man

In the teaching of Jesus the crowd discerned another kind of teaching than that of the scribes and Pharisees. «No one has ever spoken like this man» (Jn 7, 46). What distinguished him from others was above all the authority of his words: «His teaching made a deep impression on the people because he taught them with authority, unlike their own scribes» (Mt 7, 29; Mk 1, 22).

The authority of Jesus rested on many foundations. It came, certainly, from the commitment apparent in every word that he uttered. He lived out to its extreme all that he was proposing to others. He was the first to live out the demands he made.

He was not one who does not practise what he preaches. His authority was not limited to the results produced by his words, although this aspect is important[1]. It was even more evident in the way Jesus referred to the Word of God: he quoted it and dared to add with devastating simplicity: «But I say to you». Abruptly, without differentiating, he moved from the Word of God given to Moses («You have heard how it was said to our ancestors») to his own word («But I say to you»). As if God's «I» and his own were on the same level[2].

His word did not usurp God's. His «I» was never in opposition to God's. He never claimed to abolish; fulfillment was the aim he pursued (Mt 5, 17). What he claimed was to be at the heart of every Word of God, to be the one who was able to say what God expects and to speak his will for people. In this way he was able to distinguish in Scripture between what came from men's hardness of heart and what God really intended (Mk 10, 5-9). Hence his freedom regarding the Sabbath whose true meaning he established (Mt 12, 1-14; Mk 2, 23-28).

Jesus spoke in a different way from that of the scribes, and the crowds noticed. He did not surround his words with quotations from experts in Scripture. He had no recourse to human arguments. His assurance came from elsewhere; it exceeded that of the prophets and all who came before him. They too claimed to know God and his will, but they were careful to indicate the source of their assurance with the formula « thus says the Lord ». A solemn formula giving evidence that the words uttered did not derive from the one who was speaking, but from God who sent him. Jesus used a similar formula: « Amen, amen I say to you »[3], but unlike that of the prophets, this formula did not refer to someone else: it introduced words that were his own.

When Jesus spoke, it was not an intermediary between God and man who was talking. Jesus was not simply a wiser and more confident Rabbi. Gathering around Jesus to listen to his words, the crowds, says Luke, were « listening to the Word of God » (Lk 5, 1), not to a commentary on it, not to a human word. The Word made flesh (Jn 1, 14) addressed them. Between a merely human word and the teaching of Jesus, all who are listening for the Father (Jn 6, 45) discern the difference.

Jesus fulfilled the promise of the New Covenant: «They will all be taught by God» (Is 54, 13; Jn 6, 45)[4]. His authority, the authority of which the crowd was aware, was ultimately that of God, the authority given to him by the Spirit of God resting upon him (Jn 3, 34).

For many today the word «authority» poses a problem. It is often confused with authoritarianism and therefore rejected with contempt. The word of Jesus, the Word of God, is not authoritarian; it does not constrain. The power Jesus' word possesses to galvanize, to set in motion, to awaken, comes from the fact that his word reaches the intimate depths of our being, because it «speaks to the heart», to our deepest aspirations, to true freedom. It comes as a response to an expectant waiting. That is the source of his genuine authority. To awaken another to freedom, to indicate how that freedom can be attained and lived is not to constrain, it is to allow others to become themselves.

The word of Christ awakens what is deepest and truest in a human being. In contact with his word, hearts vibrate with life. Far from alienating a human being, his word alone arouses to real life. It discloses our « roots », our real « milieu » and our destiny. Staretz Zosima explains this in « The Brothers Karamazov » :

« Much on earth is hidden from us, but to make up for that we have been given a precious mystic sense of our living bond with the other world, with the higher heavenly world and the roots of our thoughts and feelings are not here but in other worlds. That is why the philosophers say that we cannot apprehend the reality of things on earth.

« God took seeds from different worlds and sowed them on this earth, and His garden grew up and everything came up that could come up, but what grows lives and is alive only through the feeling of its contact with other mysterious worlds... » [5]

At the root of our word authority is the word « author ». Jesus spoke with the authority of the Author of man. Between him and his audience there was a living bond. He is the Word, « through him all things came into being, not one thing came into being except through him»; «in him were created all things... through him and for him» (Jn 1, 3; Col 1, 16). His word, demanding, and striking in its simplicity, accords with the truth of the human heart. To love – even enemies –, to forgive, to share one's possessions and to give one's own life: no words are truer, no truth greater than this can be set before people. There is no truth more consonant with the secret aspiration of our being. That is why it is a truth that sets free (Jn 8, 32).

In Jesus, the Word of God, the human vocation can be perceived. Of Jesus it was said: «Look at the man!» (Jn 19, 5). How could his word alienate when it wears a human face to such a degree? In Christ's word man discovers himself, man is revealed:

«Not only do we know God through Jesus Christ alone, but we do not even know ourselves except through Jesus Christ. We understand life and death only through Jesus Christ. Apart from Jesus Christ we know not what is life, or our death, or God, or what we ourselves are»[6].

What we have said about the Word of God must also be said about his will, revealed by his word. Accomplishing the will of God, the Altogether Other, does not imply submitting to the arbitrary will of a stranger: it means carrying out the deepest desire of our own hearts. The woman who said: «I am the Lord's servant. May it be done to me as you have said» (Lk 1, 38), also sings: «My soul proclaims the greatness of the Lord and my spirit rejoices in God my Saviour» (Lk 1, 46-47). For the Altogether Other is never a stranger: he is, as Saint Augustine says, «deeper within me than my innermost depths» [7].

NOTES:

1. See Mk 1, 27

2. See Mt 5, 21-22; 27-28; 31-32; 33-34; 38-39; 43-44; and Lk 21, 33.

3. RSV translation: «Truly, truly, I say to you»; New Jerusalem Bible: «In all truth I tell you».

4. The basis for this text is Jr 31, 31-34.

5. DOSTOYEVSKY, *The Brothers Karamazov*, The Modern Library, Random House, New York, 1950, p. 385.

6. BLAISE PASCAL, *Pensées*, 602 (Lafuma). Notes on Religion and Other Subjects, edited with introduction and notes by Louis Lafuma, ET John Warrington, JM Dent & Sons, London, 1960, p.172.

7. *The Confessions*, III, 6, translated by V. Bourke, Catholic University of America Press, 1953. Bernanos wrote: «It is not a matter of conforming our will to his, for his will is ours, and when we rebel against it, we only cause the whole soul to be torn in hideous fragmentation. Our will has been united to his since the world began. He created the world together with us (...)» GEORGES BER-NANOS, *Journal*, Agenda, 23 January 1948.

VI

The Other and the Others

Only one text in the Gospels relates the joy experienced by Jesus in his communion with the Father. It is significant that this joy is linked with the poor and with the hope that they discover in Jesus' revelation of the Kingdom:

«At that time Jesus, full of joy through the Holy Spirit, said: 'I praise you, Father, Lord of heaven and earth, because you have hidden these things from the wise and learned, and revealed them to little children. Yes, Father, for this was your good pleasure» (Lk 10, 21).

In Matthew's version of this text, the thanksgiving of Christ is followed by an appeal: «Come to me, all you who are weary and burdened, and I will give you rest...» (Mt 11, 28). Christ's joy and his relationship with the Father are the very opposite of an escape from the world. His relationship with God is not his private matter. It does does not turn him away from others. When he rejoices, the hard realities of this world are not forgotten. Jesus is filled with joy when he sees that those who suffer, those he calls the «little ones», are finding hope. His joy arises from the fact that others, particularly those overwhelmed by heavy burdens, are discovering the value of their lives. It causes him to turn immediately towards the poor. No one has ever been in closer communion with the Father than Jesus, no one has ever been more involved in the sufferings of human beings, no one has ever been closer to others.

*

* *

For the early Christians, Christ came to establish a new communion with God but also to inaugurate a new relationship with our neighbours. And to recreate the unity of the human family. For they perceived sin not only as a break with God, but also as a break with our neighbour, a fragmentation of human unity. When they read the words in Genesis: «God created man in his own image» (1, 27), they thought of the whole human race, for «the whole of human nature from the first man to the last is but one image of him who is» (Saint Gregory of Nyssa). In the broken relationship with God, this unity of all humankind is also compromised. «And now we rend each other like the wild beasts» (Saint Maximus the Confessor). Christ, by re-establishing us in communion with God, also creates a communion in the human family: «Like the queen bee, Christ comes to muster humanity around him» (Saint Hippolytus). [1]

The Acts of the Apostles show this new communion in the making:

«The whole group of believers was united, heart and soul; no one claimed private ownership of any possessions, as everything they owned was held in common... None of their members was ever in want, as all those who owned land or houses would sell them, and bring the money from the sale of them, to present it to the apostles; it was then distributed to any who might be in need» (Ac 4, 32, 34-35).

This idealistic picture can of course be criticized and the author of the Acts himself shows that in reality such harmony did not always reign, but that a new solidarity had appeared is beyond question.

The new relationship with the Other creates new communion among humans and through this communion God himself comes and meets us: «For where two or three are gathered in my name, there I am in the midst of them» (Mt 18, 20). Where people meet and are reconciled, Christ is present.

The Altogether Other — he dwells in the communion of our sisters and brothers. The same John who wrote: «No one has ever seen God; it is the only Son, who is close to the Father's heart, who has made him known» (Jn 1, 18), also writes: «No one has ever seen God. Yet if we love one another God dwells in us, and his love is brought to perfection in us» (I Jn 4, 12). As if all love could reveal God's face, reflect the features of his Son. God, the source of all love, is present wherever someone loves.

Ubi caritas et amor Deus ibi est. *

*

* *

«What you have done, (or not done) for one of the least of these brothers of mine, you have done for me (or you have not done it)» (Mt 25, 40, 45). These words of Jesus culminate a long series of biblical texts: «On high I dwell, and in holiness, and with the crushed and dejected in spirit» the God of Israel had already said (Is 57, 15). God's nearness to the poor and his concern for them are recalled throughout the Old Testament. The God of the Bible hears the cry of the poor; he protects the foreigner and supports the widow and the orphan (Ps 146; Ex 22, 20-22). God stands close beside those who are most vulnerable, so much so that to take up

---

* Where charity and love are, God is there.

the cause of the humiliated and the poor is to know him, the Altogether Other[2].

The warning from Jesus: «See that you never despise any of these little ones, for I tell you that their angels in heaven are continually in the presence of my Father in heaven» (Mt 18, 10) furthers this line, as do several other texts: «Anyone who welcomes a little child such as this in my name, welcomes me; and anyone who welcomes me, welcomes not me but the one who sent me» (Mk 9, 37). But it is because of the Incarnation and the Cross, the source and epitome of his total identification with humankind, that Jesus can say: «What you have done for one of the least of these brothers of mine, you have done for me». Jesus can identify with everyone because «in becoming man, Christ became all men»[3]. His love embraces humankind, past, present and future. As a Council put it in the 9th Century: «There is no one who is, who was or who will be for whom Christ has not suffered»[4]. He died for all, substituting himself for others.

«By his incarnation, the Son of God has in some way united himself with every man»[5] and so it is that an encounter with the Altogether Other may arise in every chance meeting. In the poor, in particular, God himself comes to us and continually we are called to choose him. In this way the Gospel constantly challenges us. Not an alienating command but an immense and demanding challenge which calls forth our true selves. For when we neglect our responsibility for our neighbour, we not only cease to be in communion with God, we cease to be human. Without our neighbour we can have no fulfillment: «God did not create the world apart from himself, nor did he create souls apart from one another»[6].

NOTES:

1. For these three texts see, HENRI DE LUBAC, *Catholicism: A Study of Dogma in Relation to the Corporate Destiny of Mankind*, ET Lancelot C. Sheppard, New York, Longmans, Green & Co., 1950. Saint Gregory of Nyssa, p.5; Saint Maximus the Confessor, p. 7; Saint Hippolytus, p. 8.

2. See Jer 22, 16. Meditating on this fact in Scripture, EMMANUEL LÉVINAS writes: «Anyone who reveals himself as humble, on the side of the defeated, the poor, or the persecuted... is precisely not conforming to the social order (...) Breaking into immanence without fitting into it.» «Un Dieu homme?», *«Exercices de la patience»*, no. 1, 1980, p. 71.

3. Cardinal BASIL HUME, *Searching for God*, Hodder and Stoughton, 1977, p. 20.

4. Council of Quierzy (853). Quoted by Jean-Miguel Garrigues, *Dieu sans idée du mal*, Limoges, Editions Critérion, 1982, p.113.

5. *Gaudium et Spes*, par. 22, 2.

6. HENRI DE LUBAC, *op. cit.*, p. 180. On this theme, E. Lévinas quotes this text: «If I do not answer for myself, who will answer for me? But if I answer only for myself — am I still myself?» (Babylonian Talmud — Treatise Aboth 6a), *Humanisme de l'Autre Homme*, Fata Morgana, coll. Essais, 1972, p. 85

VII

Christic in Glory
One with Us

«Now about eight days after this had been said... » (Lk 9, 28)[1]. These are the opening words of the account of the Transfiguration of Jesus. In the conversation that the Gospel refers to, the identity of the Son of Man was being discussed. Jesus explained to his disciples that «the Son of Man is destined to suffer grievously, to be rejected by the elders and chief priests and scribes and to be put to death, and to be raised up on the third day» (Lk 9, 22). There is a deep unity between this announcement of his passion and his transfiguration to follow.

Jesus was transfigured, «his face changed in appearance and his clothes became dazzlingly white, whiter than the work of any bleacher could make them (Lk 9, 29; Mk 9, 3). Light not of this world clothed him and shone from him.

Beside the transfigured Jesus stood Moses and Elijah, the two great figures of the Old Testament. For a contemporary of Christ, Moses was the Law, the first books of the Bible; Elijah, the man who had suffered, the representative of the line of the prophets. Both of them are discussing the «departure of Jesus, which he was about to bring to fulfillment at Jerusalem» (Lk 9, 31). «Departure»: the word used by Luke is literally «exodus», which means «passage»; no doubt the evangelist is thinking of Jesus' passing from this world to the Father, his passing through death. This passing, this death, this giving of self are at the heart of Scripture and of the glory of Jesus: the presence of Moses and Elijah point to it, and the Risen Christ himself was to explain it to the disciples at Emmaus: «Did not the Messiah have to undergo all this so as to enter into his glory?

Beginning, then, with Moses and all the prophets, he interpreted for them every passage of Scripture which referred to him» (Lk 24, 26-27, 44).

In Saint Luke's version, it was while he was praying that Jesus was transfigured (Lk 9, 29). It was his identity as the Son turned towards the Father that shone forth. What was to be accomplished in Jerusalem was not an isolated episode in Christ's life. When he offered himself up, Jesus was faithful to what he was from the beginning, consonant with his eternal identity. Before the creation of the world (Jn 17, 24) and «setting out resolutely for Jerusalem» (Lk 9, 51), Jesus is the one who gives himself. He lives only in the mode of giving. The intense beauty shining from the transfigured Jesus, which is the sign of God's presence, what the Bible calls «glory», is the radiance of self-giving love. Not a glory consisting of impersonal, imposing importance, but the light of a face. Dazzling love.

In accepting human death, Jesus took upon himself human frailty at its most extreme. Paradoxically, glory appeared in the place of non-glory, in death. And so death was transfigured, becoming the place of the greatest love (Jn 15, 13). Nothing in the glory of Jesus rejects our poverty or towers above it; mysteriously his glory embraces and creates out of our wretchedness and the freedom we have misused. His glory is inexpressible nearness. Solidarity desired and chosen. The glory of «love crucified» shines forth at the Transfiguration[2].

*

*   *

«(...) the Nazarene made his way to the mountain. When he halted and turned round he had a nimbus of light and suffused a perfume like phlox. And he spoke of our days of shadow and his days of light as if they were the same, as if his light held something of our darkness and our darkness something of his light»[3].

NOTES:

1. Six days in Matthew and Mark.

2. The glory of solidarity is developed by the Letter to the Hebrews. «His (Christ's) glorification is presented as the consequence of his total solidarity with us even to the utmost limit of human distress. His glorification could not destroy this solidarity. On the contrary, it constitutes its definite ratification with God. The one who is glorified is our brother and he is glorified, because, according to the design of love established by God, he showed himself our brother right to the end.» ALBERT VANHOYE, *Situation du Christ, Epître aux Hébreux 1 et 2*, Paris, Cerf, coll. «Lectio Divina», no. 58, 1969, p. 341.

3. JEAN GROSJEAN, *Elie*, NRF, Gallimard, 1982, p. 115.

VIII

The Humble Servant

To evoke Christ's humility, his poverty and extreme vulnerability as they appear in the Gospel, is not to diminish his transcendence; it is to approach its dwelling-place, to draw near to the form it assumes, the places where it becomes incandescent. Taking his inspiration from human love, François Varillon has shown that humility lies at the heart of the attributes of God, even of those that appear to be the most distant. Thus the designation «the Most High» which suggests transcendence; it is not far away from humility: humility is at its very heart. A loving gaze can give us an inkling of this:

«A look of love does not lord over the one who is loved. It cannot consent to a declaration of superiority, however slight. It is humble. But through its very humility its greatness is revealed. That is why the respect evinced by the lover's humility awakens in the heart of the beloved another respect, the result and the sign of another humility. It is because not a shadow of pride darkens the gaze of the lover that his look seems to the beloved to come from far away, from *very high*, from a world which is never opaque or heavy and where there is no possibility of turning in on the self. The deeper the intimacy, the greater the distance» [1].

This is the way Christ looks at us and it is this look that lets us discover God, the Other.

*

*　　*

Jesus caused an embarrassing situation. He began to wash his disciples' feet. A curious gesture for a «Master and Lord». Washing another's feet in Jesus' day could not be asked of a Jewish slave. Sometimes a disciple would perform this service for his master. Jesus created an uncomfortable situation for his disciples; he did what one of them might have done. Icons and works of art on this scene show a murmuring of astonishment rippling through the group of disciples. Peter could not suppress his amazement: «Lord, are you going to wash my feet?... You shall never wash my feet» (Jn 13, 6,8).

Saint John introduced this gesture from Jesus with great solemnity:

«Before the festival of the Passover, Jesus, knowing that his hour had come to pass from this world to the Father, having loved those who were his in the world, loved them to the end... Jesus knew that the Father had put everything into his hands, and that he had come from God and was returning to God, and he got up from table, removed his outer garments and, taking a towel wrapped it round his waist; he then poured water into a basin and began to wash the disciples' feet and to wipe them with the towel he was wearing» (Jn 13, 1, 4-5).

A suprising juxtaposition of this decisive hour and this humble action, described down to the smallest detail. The solemn introduction invites us to enter into the profound significance of Christ's gesture. We can really only understand the act of Jesus if we first allow it to speak about God, if we remember the words of Jesus: «Anyone who has seen me has seen the Father» (Jn 14, 9). For it is above all an action which is intended to reveal God.

When he washed his disciples' feet, Jesus acted the part of a servant and so reversed the roles. Jesus revealed God to be as no one had ever imagined him. God is other than we think. When we try to imagine him, we tend to look in the direction of strength and power, something akin to domination. The Gospel shatters this image. God continues to be «Master and Lord» but the real nature of his power is revealed. He is Master by serving (Jn 13, 14). This is what Peter had to discover at all costs, otherwise he would not be in communion with Christ (Jn 13, 8). When speaking of God, he would not be talking of the God revealed by Jesus.

Jesus reveals the God who is humble. He shows how God wants to be with humanity, the manner in which God comes close to us: not by bending down from above and condescending, but by placing himself lower than we are. And in this way he reveals the infinite, the almost unbelievable respect God has for his creature; he shows how precious we are in God's sight.

A free man serves only those he loves. He acts out of pure generosity. No one is freer than Jesus. No one is freer than God. If Jesus becomes a servant, it is not because he is forced to — his life is governed by utter generosity — nor in order to play a role. Jesus is at all times perfectly himself; never is there anything factitious or artificial in his behaviour. His decision to serve his disciples springs from genuine esteem; their worth in his eyes is far greater than they can imagine.

*
*   *

At every celebration of the Eucharist, a threefold «Sanctus» reminds us that we are in the presence of the holiness of God, of the Altogether Other; at the heart of the mystery: the offering Jesus makes of his life, of his whole being. A servant to the very end, to the «full extent of love» (Jn 13, 1), he claims nothing as his own, he offers even his Body and Blood. Jesus is the Other, and that is why he is able to give himself up totally «for us»[2].

*

* *

A cohort with lanterns, torches and weapons drew near to Jesus, to arrest him (Jn 18, 3-6). He asked them: «Who are you looking for?» They answered: «Jesus the Nazarene». He said: «I am he».» And John adds: «When Jesus said to them, I am he, they moved back and fell to the ground». A surprising reaction, found in the Bible when someone witnesses a manifestation of God, when God's holiness bursts forth. By this reaction, John is saying that in this completely vulnerable, defenceless, wholly captive man, the Altogether Other is present. Christ's divinity became, as it were, incandescent at the very moment when he was «handed over into the hands of sinners», when he was at the mercy of his creatures[3].

NOTES:

1. FRANÇOIS VARILLON, *L'humilité de Dieu*, Paris, Centurion, 1974, p. 81.

2. In BONHOEFFER's words: «His (Jesus') "being there for others", is the experience of transcendence. It is only this "being there for others", maintained till death, that is the ground of his omnipotence, omniscience, and omnipresence.» *Letters and Papers from Prison*, SCM, London, 1971, p. 381.

3. On this theme, see W. H. VANSTONE, *The Stature of Waiting*, London, DLT, 1982.

IX

I Live in You

When Jesus rose from the grave he passed to a completely new life, altogether different from the one we know on earth. When it attempts to comprehend this life, the mind boggles and stammers in helplessness; the imagination wavers. But what is clear is that this life makes possible a new closeness, and enters deep into the life of all humankind. The resurrected Jesus, passing into a new life, did not distance himself from his own. He did not break the bonds of solidarity he had forged with them. The very opposite is true. It is from his resurrection that new bonds are formed, a new intimacy which is incomparably closer. The writers of the New Testament, each in his own style, emphasize this forcibly.

The Risen Christ continues to be *with* people. In Saint Luke's Gospel he is the Pilgrim who walks with his disciples on the road, who transforms their despair, sets their hearts on fire and explains the Scriptures. «With them», Luke uses these two words repeatedly when the Risen Christ is mentioned: «Stay with us... So he went in to stay with them... When he was at the table with them...» (Lk 24, 29-30). The Risen Christ is the one who is *with*. And Matthew adds that he would remain so «to the end of time» (Mt 28, 20), fulfilling the promise made in the opening chapter of his Gospel: «Immanuel, God-is-with-us» (1, 23).

For John, the Risen Christ makes himself closer still. New bonds are formed and a new relationship is inaugurated with which no human relationship can be compared. Jesus is no longer simply with the disciples, he is now «in them» (Jn 17, 26); in them, together with his Father, he makes his home (Jn 14, 23). The new relationship can only be compared with that which Jesus has with his Father: «I pray also for those who will believe in me through their message, that all of them may be one, Father, just as you are in me and I am in you. May they also be in us... I have given them the glory that you gave me, that they may be one as we are one: I in them and you in me» (Jn 17, 21-23).

This new proximity which was to come with the resurrection is illustrated by John in the image of the vine (Jn 15), a well-known image in the Old Testament. For the Prophets the vine was the chosen people, planted by God and surrounded by his care and his protection, but in the end producing nothing but bitter fruit (Is 5, 2). We must capture the sadness and disappointment associated with the vine-theme in Scripture to catch the note of joy in the voice of Jesus when he said: «I am the vine... Whoever remains in me, with me in him, bears fruit in plenty» (Jn 15, 5). God did his utmost for his people to bear fruit, but to no avail. All he could do now was to become the vine himself, uniting himself with the human race in order to carry it entirely. In Christ God united himself so intimately with humanity that it is impossible to separate them: being the

Vine, he is present in the wood, the sap and the fruits. In him takes place the «marvellous exchange» begun at Christmas and which, through Christ's passing through death, was enriched with new depth. «God was made man in order that we might become God» the early Christians loved to repeat, in wonder at the complete sharing established between God and us in Christ.

To continue what he had begun Jesus communicated to his disciples his own Breath (Jn 20, 22). He promised to be present in their endeavours: «All authority in heaven and on earth has been given to me. Go, therefore...» (Mt 28, 18-19).

If the resurrection, and more particularly Christ's Ascension, have sometimes been confused with an absence or remoteness, a superficial reading of Saint John and a too literal interpretation of the Ascension are probably at fault. When John says that Jesus is going away, it must not be taken to imply that the Risen Christ has gone away – for his departure is a coming. «His departure is the opposite of an abandonment of the disciples; Jesus comes to them as result of his departure». «Our Lord was to disappear, but only in order to make himself seen»[1]. «I am going away and I am coming back to you.» «I will not leave you as orphans; I will come to you» (Jn 14, 28, 18).

When Jesus ascends into heaven, it is neither to distance himself nor to disappear. Saint Luke writes that after the disciples saw Jesus ascend, they «went back to Jerusalem full of joy; and they were continually in the Temple praising God» (Lk 24, 52-53). They were not filled with the sadness of departure. They understood that from now on, Christ would be closer still to them, his presence would be more active and more universal. «The fact that Jesus Christ is now within the Father is why we perceive him so much the more clearly», a second century Christian[2] was bold enough to declare. And both Saint John and Saint Paul agree with him, for the Father to whom Jesus has ascended is not far away: «He is within all» (Ep 4, 6; Jn 14, 23).

To translate the new proximity issuing from the resurrection of Jesus, the Gospel attributes to the disciples a new name: they

89

are called his «brothers». «Go and tell my brothers that they must leave for Galilee; there they will see me» (Mt 28, 10). «Go and find my brothers, and tell them: I am ascending to my Father and your Father, to my God and your God» (Jn 20, 17). The author of the Letter to the Hebrews insists on this new name, for more than anyone else he emphasizes Christ's solidarity with us.

«I will announce your name to my brothers, I will sing your praise in the midst of the assembly» (Heb 2, 12), sings the Risen Christ of the Letter to the Hebrews[3]. His hymn is a verse of Psalm 22, the very psalm Jesus began to say on the cross: «My God, my God, why have you abandoned me?» and which inspired more than any other text the accounts of the Passion. Jesus takes up this same psalm when he has risen, for this Old Testament text ends with the delivrance of the sufferer. It is this psalm which seems to have inspired the Gospel-writers themselves in their use of the word brother[4].

Psalm 22 reports the trials of an innocent man who is suffering in painful loneliness. No one is there to help him. There is nothing around but hostility and mockery. When God intervenes in his favour and saves him, he would be entirely justified to reject and abandon those who tormented and forsook him. In the psalm, however, there is nothing of the sort. Once healed and returned to life, the psalmist affirms his solidarity with the whole human family and he expresses himself with an astonishing universality, as if the life God had given back to him had to flow and spread out over the whole world, to everybody's benefit. To join in his praise should come: «the race of Israel», the «poor», «all who seek God», «the whole wide world», «all the families of the nations», even the dead (v. 30), «generations still to come», «peoples yet unborn».

This psalm of solidarity – the greatest of them all, – is the one sung by the Risen Christ in the Letter to the Hebrews. By means of this psalm whose opening was proclaimed by Jesus, together with two other quotations from the Old Testament, the Letter to the Hebrews presents us with a kind of image of the Church. Christ is at the centre proclaiming God's name to his brothers, «in the midst of the assembly»[5]. Now that he is saved from death and from all that threatens him, he proclaims that he is sure of God: «I will put my trust in him». But to show that Christ remains close to us, that he shares his assurance with us, another quotation is added to the first, which otherwise could seem too individual: «Here am I, and the children God has given me» (Heb 2, 12-13). The confidence that we receive because Jesus is risen is not drawn uniquely from ourselves; it is more than a psychological disposition: it arises from the very presence of Christ in us, Christ who assumed the darkness of the human condition and remained certain of the faithfulness of God.

The Risen Christ, the anchor reaching right through inside the curtain (Heb 6, 19), firmly fixed by unbreakable cords to the ship that we are, is the promise of our resurrection (I Co 15, 20). He is «the first-born from the dead» (Col 1, 18). Our resurrection − it is impossible to imagine it! And it is not the Jesus of the Gospels who would encourage us to do so, for just as much as the Sadducees, we underestimate «the power of God» (Mt 22, 23-33). The reality of the resurrection surpasses all imagining; it is not of this world. But the Gospel teaches that the Resurrection is Someone (Jn 11, 25); and we know, even better than Job, that on that day our «eyes will be gazing on no stranger» (Job 19,27).

NOTES:

1. F.-X. DURWELL, *La Résurrection de Jésus, Mystère de Salut*, 10th edition, Paris, Cerf, 1976, p. 101; *The Resurrection: A Biblical Study*, ET Rosemary Sheed, New York: Sheed & Ward, 1960, p. 205. The first quotation is my translation of the French edition.

2. SAINT IGNATIUS OF ANTIOCH , *The Epistle to the Romans, 3*, translated by Maxwell Staniforth, *The Early Christian Writings*, Penguin Books, 1968, p.104.

3. On Hebrews see A. VANHOYE, *Situation du Christ, Hébreux 1 et 2*, Paris, Cerf, Coll. Lectio Divina 1969.

4. *Ibid.*, p. 340.

5. The word used here is *ekklèsia*, which gives us our word Church.

X

The Spirit Prays Within Us

Jesus promises the Holy Spirit to his disciples. Another Paraclete, someone who will be concerned about them, who will take charge of them, of all that they are, all they require, who will always be at their side, who will watch over them, taking care of their needs and defending them.

The Paraclete will be present in such a way that the disciples need have no anxiety. He will recall everything to their memory (Jn 14, 26). He will be within them to give witness[1]. He will tell them, not something new, but all that is Christ's: «all he reveals to you will be taken from what is mine» (Jn 16, 14).

To every age, and to every person, the Spirit communicates the life of Christ; the Spirit makes it personal within each one. Christ is never far away in time; we do not know him at second hand, nor by great efforts of clambering over the centuries separating us from a distant era – the Spirit makes him known to us. By the Spirit the words of Jesus come to life; they are addressed to each one of us. The Spirit weaves a tie straight from Christ to every believer. More than that, the Spirit makes Christ our very life to the point where we can say: «I no longer live, but Christ lives in me» (Ga 2, 20). But anyone who accepts the life of Christ is not dispossessed of his true self nor deprived of his personality. Being guided by the Spirit does not mean becoming robots. Quite the contrary. The Spirit causes «our constant reference to Christ and the very life of Christ within us to be our most personal inspiration.» «With infinite discretion he causes Christ to live in me and I am in no way dislodged: quite the contrary, I become more truly myself and free»[2].

Reflecting on the inspiration of the

Gospels can help us to realize this work of the Spirit in us. We know Christ by means of four gospels. We say that all are inspired by the one Spirit and yet they reflect different points of view and each evidences specific concerns. But this diversity takes nothing away from the inspired character of each gospel. Rather, it shows that in order to speak through human beings, the Spirit does not destroy their personalities. The Spirit never turns these men, nor any of us, into mere tools. When he inspires the Gospel-writers, the Spirit does not empty them of what they are: he enhances their own characters, developing their gifts and guiding them into fulfilment. The Spirit is present in the intellectual efforts of each evangelist and in the concern of each to be understood by his readers. Under the inspiration of the Spirit, John becomes more John, Matthew more Matthew etc. The Spirit makes use of the four personalities of the Gospel-writers and their four points of view to transmit, as he wills, the riches of the mystery of Christ.

*

*　　　*

It is perhaps because we have not paid sufficient attention to the role of the Holy Spirit that God has often appeared an alienating presence. God is not far from our thirsting. The Holy Spirit is the Author of every desire for fullness. In the groaning of creation and of every human being, it is the Holy Spirit animating our aspiration for freedom. And the Spirit draws us to the place where it can find fulfilment; the Spirit whispers: «Come to the Father»[3].

To discover the Holy Spirit is to discover that God is not only the Other facing us. God the Spirit is already present within us through the desire to encounter the Father and the Son, and the Spirit takes part in this encounter with us, from our side, so to speak. He comes to help us in our weakness. He prays within us (Rm 8, 26-27)[4]. With the Bride, the Spirit says: «Come!» (Rv 22, 17). He reveals the splendour of the communion of love existing between the Father and the Son and the place prepared for us that we may share in it.

*

*　　*

98

For many Christians any reference to the Spirit creates a problem. The Spirit is so unimaginable! When the Father is spoken of, some are helped by the image conjured up by the word father (this is a hindrance to others); for Jesus, the Gospel sketches a face and presents human features — but the Spirit cannot be captured, he is as elusive as the wind. What face can be given to a breath or a fire? The Spirit is indeed the Other. He is not of this world. And yet, if everything impels us to say «there is nothing less earthly than the Spirit», we discover also in him a complete «fidelity to those earthly realities he has chosen: the bread and wine of the Eucharist, the life of the believer, the gatherings of men and women in which the Church takes visible form» [5], human love and our mortal bodies which he will raise (Rm 8, 11). The Spirit rejects nothing that is human. He is present in our stammering prayers, in our desire, and has his home in the poor words of men and women who try to bear witness to Christ. Altogether Other and thus Altogether Close.

NOTES:

1. Mt 10, 20; Mk 13, 11; Lk 12, 12; Jn 15, 26.

2. BROTHER PIERRE-YVES of Taizé, *Le Saint Esprit, Présence de Communion*, Les Presses de Taizé, 1980, p.50.

3. SAINT IGNATIUS OF ANTIOCH, The Epistle to the Romans, 7, translated by Maxwell Staniforth, *The Early Christian Writings*, Penguin Books, 1968, p.106.

4. « In the person of Jesus, and in his body, the church, the Spirit calls all men to respond. And like a fifth column in the heart of every man the Spirit himself moves in response. » JOHN TAYLOR, *The Go-Between God*, SCM, 1972, p. 181.

5. BROTHER PIERRE-YVES of Taizé, *op. cit.*, p.217.

Astonishment,
Wonder and Praise

«His art of being other,
that is to say, to astonish».
France Quéré

Because he never ceases to elude our categories, because he surpasses all expectation, because in «bringing himself he has brought all newness» (Saint Irenaeus), the God of the Gospel is discovered only in astonishment: «Who can this be?» (Mk 4, 41). «Nothing like this has ever been seen in Israel!» (Mt 9, 33). «No one has ever spoken like this man!» (Jn 7, 46).

And yet a long period of ardent, eager expectation prepared for the coming of Christ. Prophets announced him and foretold his destiny by their oracles; they prepared his way and proclaimed the

101

divine plan that he would come and accomplish, and yet when he appeared, he upset even the most alert of the watchful:

«Surprise is one of the chief elements in the coming of the expected Christ. One could indeed object that, to complete a programme (in biblical terms a plan), or else to resemble a model, does not bring with it the shock of newness, that it is more similar to repetitiveness, fixity and finally boredom. But whether it is a question of conforming to the programme or the portrait, discovering him for the witnesses of the Gospel is discovering something unheard of. The resemblance is hidden because it was not discovered immediately. That is a stronger paradox than an «ordinary paradox», one might perhaps say: a more paradoxical paradox. And so the Gospel brought and brings joyful news: he has come, the unknown one I was expecting» [1].

Astonishment lies in seeing him appear where no one would ever have dared expect him, in his choice to bind himself to our wretchedness and take the place of a servant. If he appears as the Other, it is not because he is distant or far away but because he makes himself incredibly close: «You come to me!» cries John the

Baptist. « You, Lord! Wash my feet? » asks Peter. « This man welcomes sinners and eats with them » exclaim the Pharisees.

Wonder arises also from the presence of God in a man, in someone more human than we are. In the existence of Jesus, defenceless and vulnerable. In the fact that forgiveness and the will of Another are transmitted by his gestures and his word, by his most intimate *I*. In him who is so close to us, who is one of us, in his sensitivity and his spontaneity, the Altogether Other is present. The one so close to us is the Other.

Drawing near to all that comes from the God of the Gospel is possible only through wonder. Otherwise how can we confess these truths of the faith: the Master has made himself a Servant, the Word has become flesh[2], God is present in the humble bread and wine we bring to him, Christ is risen!

Astonishment, wonder, but also that other reality that God leaves in his wake as he passes — praise. For the wonder of the believer is born in the discovery of God's nearness. To wonder is to *see*[3], to glimpse

103

an immense and active solicitude, to behold love in action. The realisation of being included in a kindly plan causes gratitude to well up, in response to God's free gift:

«Blessed be God the Father of our Lord Jesus Christ, who has blessed us with all the spiritual blessings of heaven in Christ. Thus he chose us in Christ, before the world was made, to be holy and faultless before him in love, marking us out for himself beforehand, to be adopted sons, through Jesus Christ. Such was his purpose and good pleasure, to the praise of the glory of his grace, his free gift to us in the Beloved» (Ep 1, 3-6).

Astonishment and praise, two realities that seem remarkably united in the stories surrounding the birth of Jesus, a prelude to what his life on earth was to awaken. The wonderment of Mary at the angel's announcement (Lk 1, 29) echoed by the jubilation of the Magnificat. (Lk 1, 46-55). Uniting both astonishment and gratitude, Elisabeth's question: «why I am so favored, that the mother of my Lord should come to me?» (Lk 1, 43), which means: is it possible that God could be so good? The «great fear» of the shepherds (Lk 2, 9) at the announcement of the birth of Jesus, their visit to the child and their return full of praise: «the shepherds went back glorifying and praising God for all they had heard and seen, just as they had been told» (Lk 2, 20).

Astonishment, wonder and praise are what the newness of Christ provoke, but also, according to an ancient text, astonishment and peace: «Let anyone who is seeking cease not until he find. And when he finds he will be astonished. Astonished he shall find the kingdom and having found the kingdom he shall rest» [4]. Astonishment and peace — an impossible marriage? Not so. Certainly the revolution introduced by the Gospel is real, and none greater exists, since it asks man to be born again (Jn 3, 3), but this revolution and this birth introduce us to our real depth; being born to God, we are also born ourselves; we become alive. Our secret expectancy finds a response. If the Gospel disorientates it is only in order to reorientate us towards the true fullness of life. It is so that serene jubilation can be born.

Such is the God of the Gospel, surprising even with regard to the Scriptures
that prepared his coming, such in one
sense is the Christian faith with regard to
man: it finds in his heart a mooring-point
and correspondence, responding to his
genuine expectancy, to all his aspirations
and it is at the same time «what no mind
had conceived» (I Co 2, 9).

Wonder, which rises from the presence of the Altogether Other and his newness. Peace, because this Other, the opposite of a stranger, is «deeper within me
than my innermost depths».

*

* *

«There is only one face which is absolutely beautiful – the face of Christ, and
the appearance of this infinitely, incom-
mensurably beautiful face, is an endless
miracle». [5]

NOTES:

1. PAUL BEAUCHAMP, *Psaumes nuit et jour*, Paris, Ed. du Seuil, 1980, p. 40.

2. SAINT AUGUSTINE: «The wisdom of God was revealed in the features of a baby, and the Word of God whimpered in the flesh.» «He who contains the world was lying in a manger, both an infant without speech, and at the same time the Word.» KIERKEGAARD: «Anyone who does not give up the criterion of likelihood never enters into relationship with God.» DOSTOYEVSKY: «The truth is unlikely».

3. The Greek word for wonder contains the notion of sight.

4. A Christian text of the second century, quoted by CLEMENT OF ALEXANDRIA.

5. DOSTOYEVSKY, *Correspondence, III*, Paris, Calmann-Lévy, p.173.

The Taizé Community

«A PARABLE OF COMMUNION»

August 1940, with Europe in the grip of World War II, Brother Roger, aged 25, set up home in the almost abandoned village of Taizé, in Eastern France. His dream: to bring together a monastic community which would live out "a parable of community", a parable to be set at the heart of the distress of the time. Centering his life on prayer, he used his house to conceal refugees, especially Jews fleeing from the Nazi occupation.

AN INTERNATIONAL ECUMENICAL COMMUNITY

Taizé's founder spent the first two years alone. Others joined him later and at Easter 1949, seven brothers committed themselves together in the common life and celibacy. Year by year, still others have entered the community, each one making a lifelong commitment after several years of preparation. Today, there are 90 brothers, Catholics and from various Protestant backgrounds, from over twenty different coun-

109

tries. Some of them are living in small "fraternities" in poor neighbourhoods in Asia, Africa, North and South America. The brothers accept no donations or gifts for themselves, not even family inheritances, and the community holds no capital. The brothers earn their living and share with others entirely through their own work.

In 1966, Sisters of Saint Andrew, an international Catholic community founded 750 years ago, came to live in the neighbouring village, to share the responsibility of welcoming people in Taizé.

TAIZÉ AND THE YOUNG:
THE INTERCONTINENTAL MEETINGS

Young people, and less young, have been coming to Taizé in ever greater numbers since 1957. Hundreds of thousands of people from Europe and far beyond have thus been brought together in a common search. Intercontinental meetings take place each week, Sunday to Sunday, throughout the year and they include youth from between 35 and 60 countries during any one week. The meetings give each person the opportunity to explore the wellsprings of faith and to reflect on how to unite the inner life and human solidarity.

The meetings in summer can have up to 6,000 participants a week, while in spring and autumn there are between 500 and 1,000. The greatest numbers gather at Easter, Pentecost and All Saints.

Three times every day, the brothers and everybody on the hill come together for common prayer in the Church of Reconciliation, built in 1962 when the church in the village became too small.

« THE PILGRIMAGE OF TRUST ON EARTH »

The community has never wanted to create a «movement» around itself and young people are called rather to commit themselves in their church at home, in their neighbourhood, their city or village, or in their parish. To support them in this, Taizé is animating "a pilgrimage of trust on earth". At the end of each year, the pilgrimage has a "European meeting" which brings together tens of thousands of young adults from every part of Europe for several days in a major city. There are also "Asian meetings" (India and the Philippines) Every year, Brother Roger writes an open letter to young people. Usually completed during a stay in one of the poor regions of the world, these are translated into thirty languages and provide themes for reflexion for the following year.

Address: The Taizé Community, 71250 Cluny, France
Tel: Community (33) 85.50.30.30.
Meetings (33) 85.50.30.02.
Fax: (33) 85.50.30.15 Tlx: 800753 COTAIZE

ACHEVÉ D'IMPRIMER
EN JUIN 1991
SUR LES PRESSES DE TAIZÉ
71250 - TAIZÉ (FRANCE)

Dépôt légal : juillet 1991 – N° 743 – Les Presses de Taizé